What We Have in Common

A Brim Coloring Book

Written by Jane Landey
Edited by David Austin
Drawings by David Austin and Jane Austin

Published by CreateSpace: An Amazon Company.
Printed in U.S.A.

Introduction

What We Have in Common. Brim Coloring Books enable children to color the drawings as they read along! They display the similarities of related animals. In this series, the dog and the fox are compared. The facts enable children to appreciate common values. Thus, imbibing in them interest towards animals which could help them appreciate what they have in common with one another.

The Dog

And

The Fox

The dog and the fox have many things in common.
They look alike and are flesh eaters.
Dogs live with people while Foxes live in the forest.

A dog and a fox meet in the woods.

I am a dog.

I am a fox.

I have four limbs.

I have four limbs too!

And I have a long tail.

I have a long tail too!

I have two eyes.

I have two eyes too!

I have pointed ears.

I have pointed ears too!

My teeth are strong and sharp for eating bones.

I eat bones with my sharp teeth too!

I smell with my nose.

Me too!

I have puppies.

I have pups too!

I play with my puppies.

I play with my pups too!

Mister Dog and Mister Fox talk behind the wall.

Mister Dog is with Mister Fox.

Mister Dog kneels before Mister Fox.

Mister Dog is hiding behind trees.

Mister Fox is hiding behind trees too!

Both are saying good bye.

Mister Fox is going back into the forest.

Mister Dog is going back home.

It is getting dark. Mister Fox is running.

Mister Dog walks on. He lives in a cottage with its puppies.

Mister Fox lives in a hole with its pups.

Mister Dog goes away.

Mister Fox goes away.

What We Have in Common Brim Coloring Books

Crocodile and Alligator
Turtle and Tortoise
Starfish and Octopus
Worm and Snake
Vulture and Turkey
Ostrich and Emu
Weka and Kiwi
Bat and Rat
Camel and Llama
Duck and Pelican
Kangaroo and Wallaby
Pig and Tapir
Skunk and Squirrel
Hedge and Anteater
Cat and Owl
Elephant and Rhinoceros
Dog and Fox
Buffalo and Bull
Tiger and Cheetah
Horse and Zebra

www.ingramcontent.com/pod-product-compliance
Lightning Source LLC
Chambersburg PA
CBHW080817280726
48660CB00018B/3496